With Christmas In Mind

This publicat...
the Uni...

Exclusive Distributors:

Music Sales Limited

8/9 Frith Street, London W1V 5TZ, England.

Music Sales Pty Limited

120 Rothschild Avenue, Rosebery, NSW 2018, Australia.

Order No. AM945747

ISBN 0-86001-062-7

This book © Copyright 1997 by Wise Publications.

Compiled by Peter Evans & Peter Lavender.

Your Guarantee of Quality:
As publishers, we strive to produce every book to the highest commercial standards.
This book has been carefully designed to minimise awkward page turns and to make playing from it a real pleasure.
Particular care has been given to specifying acid-free, neutral-sized paper made
from pulps which have not been elemental chlorine bleached.
This pulp is from farmed sustainable forests and was produced with special regard for the environment.
Throughout, the printing and binding have been planned to ensure a sturdy,
attractive publication which should give years of enjoyment.
If your copy fails to meet our high standards, please inform us and we will gladly replace it.

Music Sales' complete catalogue describes thousands of titles and
is available in full colour sections by subject, direct from Music Sales Limited.
Please state your areas of interest and send a cheque/postal order for £1.50 for postage to:
Music Sales Limited, Newmarket Road, Bury St. Edmunds, Suffolk IP33 3YB.

Printed in Great Britain by
Printwise (Haverhill) Limited, Haverhill, Suffolk

When Santa Got Stuck Up The Chimney

Words & Music by Jimmy Grafton

Merry Christmas Everybody

Words & Music by Neville Holder & James Lea

— ies keep_ him so - ber for_ a day?_____
and rock_ 'n' roll - in' with the best_____
— up - on your head___ then you___ bin slayed!_____

So hear it

Am   E   Am   C(+9)   D4   D   C   D

CHORUS

is   mer - ry   Christ - mas   ev - 'ry - bo - dy's   hav - ing   fun_____

G   Bm7   Bb   D

Look   to the   fu - ture   now_   it's   on - ly   just   be - gun._____

G   Bm7   Bb   D

1
_____ Are you wait-_____

2
What will your dad - dy do___ when he sees your Ma -

Interlude

Dm   Bb

D. S. al Coda

-ma kiss-in' San - ta Claus? Ah ah!_____ Are you hang-

Dm   Bb   C   D

CODA

is mer-ry Christ - mas ev - 'ry - bo - dy's hav-ing fun_____

G   Bm7   Bb   D

Look   to the fu - ture now___ it's on - ly just be - gun_____

G   Bm7   Bb

_____ so   here   it   on - ly just be - gun_____

rit.   molto

D   C D   Bb   D

8

Winter Wonderland

Words by Dick Smith
Music by Felix Bernard

an-y old time, Here in the o - pen, we're walk-in' and hop-in' to-geth-er! ____

Eb   Bb7   Eb   Cm   F7   Bb7   Eb   Fm7 Bb7

CHORUS

Sleigh bells ring, are you list-'nin'! In the lane snow is glist-'nin', A

Lightly   p–f

Eb   Bb7   Fm Bb7

beau-ti-ful sight, We're hap-py to-night, walk_in' in a win-ter won-der-land! Gone a-way is the

F9   Bb7   Eb

blue-bird, Here to stay is a new bird, He sings a love-song, As we go a-long,

Bb7   Fm Bb7

walk - in' in a win-ter won-der - land! —   In the mea-dow we can build a snow-man,

F9   Db7   Eb   G   D7   G

Then pre-tend that he is Par-son Brown,   He'll say "Are you married?" we'll say, "No, man! But

D7   G   Bb   F9   Bb

you can do the job when you're in town!" — La-ter on we'll con-spire As we dream by the fire — To

C9   F7   Bb7   Eb   Bb7   Fm Bb7

1   2   𝄋

face un-a-fraid, the plans that we made,   walk-in' in a win-ter won-der land!   Sleigh bells -land! —

F9   Bb7   Eb   Bb7   Eb   D.S.

11

Mary's Boy Child

Words & Music by Jester Hairston

Long time a-go in Beth-le-hem so the Ho-ly Bi-ble say,

Ma-ry's Boy Child, Je-sus Christ was born on Christ-mas Day

REFRAIN

Hark, now hear the an-gels sing, a new King born to-day, And

Man will live for ev-er-more, Be-cause of Christ-mas Day. Trum-pets sound and

an - gels sing, list - en to what they say, That Man will live for

3rd time to ✧ Coda

ev - er - more, Be - cause of Christ-mas Day. While

By and

shep-herds watched their flocks by night, them see a bright new shin-ing star, Them
by they find a lit - tle nook in a sta - ble all for-lorn, And

13

hear a choir sing, the mus- ic seemed to come from a - far. Now Jo-seph and his
in a man-ger cold anddark,Ma-ry's lit-tle Boy was born. Long time a-go in

wife, Ma - ry, come to Beth-le-hem that night, Them find no place to born she Child, Not a
Beth-le-hem, so the Ho-ly Bi-ble say, — Ma-ry's Boy Child, Je-sus Christ,was

D.S. 𝄋   ⊕ CODA

sin- gle room was in sight.
born on Christ-mas Day.

D.S. 𝄋

Day.— Be- cause of Christ-mas

ten.

ten.

rall.   -   -   -

Day.

a tempo

mp
rit.

Ped. _____ *

Carol Of The Drum

Words & Music by Katherine K. Davis

Moderato

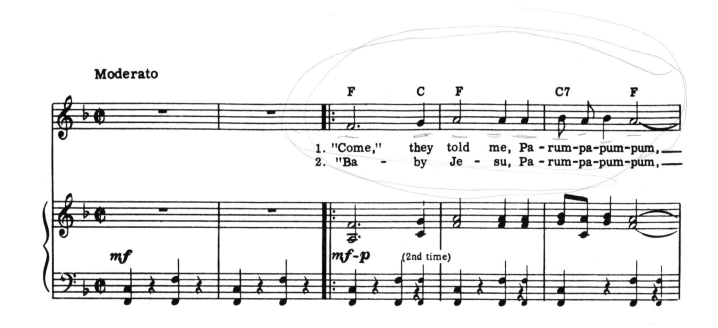

1. "Come," they told me, Pa - rum-pa-pum-pum,
2. "Ba - by Je - su, Pa - rum-pa-pum-pum,

— "Our new-born King to see! Pa - rum-pa-pum-pum,
— I'm a poor boy too, Pa - rum-pa-pum-pum,

Our fin - est gifts we'll bring, Pa - rum-pa-pum-pum, ____ To lay be -
I have no gift to bring, Pa - rum-pa-pum-pum, ____ That's fit to

fore the King! Pa - rum-pa-pum-pum,   Rum-pa-pum-pum,   Rum-pa-pum-pum, ____

give a King, Pa - rum-pa-pum-pum,   Rum-pa-pum-pum,   Rum-pa-pum-pum, ____

So to hon-or Him, Pa-rum-pa-pum-pum, ____   When we come" ____

Shall I play for you, Pa-rum-pa-pum-pum, ____   on __ my drum?" __

1. (Tacet)   2. (Tacet)

3. Mar - y nod - ded, Pa-

rum-pa-pum-pum, ____   Ox and ass kept time, Pa-rum-pa-pum-pum, ____

16

Sleigh Ride

Words by Mitchell Parish
Music by Leroy Anderson

up to-geth-er like two birds of a feath-er would be. _____ Let's take that road be-fore us and

Am7   G   B♭ D7   G

sing a cho-rus or two, _____ Come on, it's love-ly weath-er for a SLEIGH RIDE to-geth-er with

Am7 D7   G   Am7 D7   G   Am7   D7

1 | To Interlude ‖ 2 Last time

you. _____   There's a   you. _____

G C G   C G   D7   G

INTERLUDE

birth-day par-ty   at the home of Farm — er Gray,   It-'ll   be the per-fect

Gmaj7
(D6)

end — ing   of a   per — fect   day,   We'll   be   sing-ing the   songs we

G#dim

20

love to sing with-out a sin-gle stop, At the fire-place while we

Am7   A#dim   G   B7   Em   B   Em6

watch the chest-nuts pop.   POP! POP! POP! There's a hap-py feel-ing noth-ing in the

C#m7   F#7   B   G#dim   D7   Gmaj
(D6)

world can buy, When they pass a-round the cof-fee and the pump-kin

pie, It-'ll near-ly be like a pic-ture print by Cur-ri-er and Ives,

G#dim   Am7   A#dim   G   B7   Em   A7

These won-der-ful things are the things we re-mem-ber all thru our lives! Just hear those

D   C   D   C   D   C   D   C   D

D.S. al Fine

21

Wonderful Christmastime

Words & Music by McCartney

ooh, _____ ooh, _____

Do do, do do, do do do.

We're

simp - ply hav - ing a wonder - ful Christ-mas time. time.

Cm7 F Dm(sus Eb) Gm Eb Ab9 1 Bb 2 Bb D.%. al Coda

25

sim - ply hav - ing a won-der-ful Christmas time. (We're) sim - ply

hav - ing a won-der-ful Christ-mas time. time. Oh _____

_____ Oh _____

_____ Oh Christ-mas time. _____

dim. poco a poco

26

Last Christmas

Words & Music by George Michael

give it to some-one spe-cial. Last Christ-mas I gave you my heart,_ but the

ve-ry next day you gave it a-way._ This year_ to save me from tears_ I'll

give it to some-one spe-cial.

§ to fade

Once bit-ten and
A crowd-ed room,

The Little Boy That Santa Claus Forgot

Words & Music by Tommie Connor, Michael Carr & Jimmy Leach

CHORUS

Have Yourself A Merry Little Christmas

Words & Music by Hugh Martin & Ralph Blane

I Believe In Father Christmas

Words by Peter Sinfield
Music by Greg Lake

1. They said there'll be
2. They sold me a

snow at Christ-mas, They said there'll be peace on earth;
dream of Christ-mas, They sold me a sil-ent night;

G/D   D   G/D   D   G/D   D

But in-stead it just kept on rain-ing A veil of tears for the
and they told me a fair-y sto-ry Till I be-lieved in the

Vir-gin birth.___ I re-mem-ber one Christ-mas morn-ing___ A
Is-rael-ite___ and I be-lieved in Fa-ther Christ-mas,— And I

win-ter's light__and a dis-tant choir,___ And the peal of a bell and that
looked to the sky with ex-ci-ted eyes,___ Till I woke with a yawn in the

Christ-mas tree smell,__ And their eyes full of tin-sel and fire.___
first light of dawn,__ And I saw him and through his dis-guise.___

G/D D G/D D G/D D
G/D D Am7/D G/D D
Am7/D G/D D
G/D D

3 I wish you a hopeful Christmas
  I wish you a brave New Year
  All anguish, pain and sadness
  Leave your heart and let your road be clear.
  They said there'd be snow at Christmas
  They said there'd be peace on earth
  Hallelujah Noel be it heaven or hell
  The Christmas we get we deserve.

Saviour's Day

Words & Music by Chris Eaton

Life can be yours if you on - ly stay, _____ He is calling you, calling you_ on the Sa-viour's

Day, on the Sa-viour's Day, on the Sa-viour's

Day, (He_____ is call - ing__ you __ on the Sa-viour's
      (on the Sa-viour's Day.

Repeat to Fade

call -ing, call - ing, call - ing you. Call-ing call -ing call-ing you.
Raise up your glas - ses and drink to the King. Raise up your glas-ses and drink to the

Santa Claus Is Comin' To Town

Words by Haven Gillespie
Music by J. Fred Coot

CHORUS (*delicato*)

bad or good, So be good for good-ness sake. Oh! You bet-ter watch out, you bet-ter not cry,

G   G#dim   Am7   D7   G   Gaug7   C   C7   F   Fm

Bet-ter not pout, I'm tell-ing you why: San-ta Claus is com-in' to town.   With

C   C7   F   Fm   C   Am7   Dm7   G   C   G7

Music Box Chorus

lit-tle tin horns and lit-tle toy drums, Root-y-toot-toots and rum-my-tum-tums, San-ta Claus is

C   F   C   F   Fm   C

com-in'   to   town.   And cur-ly head dolls that tod-dle and coo,

G7   C   G7   C   F

El - e - phants, boats and kid-die cars too, San-ta Claus is com-in' to town. ____ The

Kids in Girl - and Boy - land will have a jub - i - lee, ____ They're gon - na build a

Toy-land town all a - round the Christ-mas tree, So! You bet-ter watch out, you bet-ter not cry,

Bet - ter not pout, I'm tell - ing you why: San-ta Claus is com-in' to town. ____

Christmas Alphabet

Words & Music by Buddy Kaye & Jules Loman

CHORUS (*moderately slow*)

"C" is for the can-dy trimmed a-round the Christ-mas tree. "H" is for the hap-pi-ness with all the fam-i-ly. "R" is for the rein-deer pranc-ing by the win-dow pane. "I" is for the ic-ing on the cake as sweet as su-gar cane. "S" is for the stock-ing

on the chim-ney wall.   "T" is for the toys   be-neath the tree so tall.   "M" is for the mis-tle-toe where

ev-'ry-one is kissed.   "A" is for the an-gels who make   up the Christ-mas list.

"S" is for old San-ta who makes ev-'ry kid his pet.   Be good and he'll bring you ev-'ry-thing in   your

1.
Christ-mas al - pha-bet.

2.
Christ-mas al - pha-bet.

47

Baby It's Cold Outside

Words & Music by Frank Loesser

48

nice_____ My moth-er will start to wor-ry_____ And
warm_____ My sis-ter will be sus-pic-ious_____ My

I'll hold your hands They're just like ice_____ Beau-ti-ful, what's your
Look out the win-dow at that storm_____ Gosh, your lips look de -

fath - er will be pac-ing the floor_____ So real-ly I'd bet-ter
broth - er will be there at the door_____ My maid-en aunts' mind is

hur - ry?_____ Lis-ten to the fi-re-place roar!
li - cious_ Waves up-on a trop-ic-al shore!

scur - ry._____ Well, may-be just a half a drink more_____ The
vic - ious _ Well, may-be just a ci-ga-rette more_____ I've

Beau - ti-ful, please,don't hur-ry Put some re-cords on while I pour
Gosh, your lips are de - li-cious Nev-er such a bliz-zard be-fore

neigh-bors might think _____ Say, What's in this drink? _____
got to get home _____ Say, lend me a comb _____

— But, ba - by, it's bad __ out there __ No cabs to be had ____
— But, ba - by, you'd freeze out there __ It's up to your knees __

— I wish I knew how _____ to break the
— You've real - ly been grand _____ but don't you

out there __ Your eyes are like star - light now __
out there __ I thrill when you touch __ my hand __

spell _____ I ought to say "No, no,
see _____ There's bound to be talk to -

I'll take your hat __ your hair looks swell _____
How can you do __ this thing to me _____

50

no, Sir!"___ At least I'm gon-na say that I tried _____ I
mor-row.__ At least there will be plen-ty im - plied _____ I

Mind if I move in clos-er?___ What's the sense of hurt-ing my pride___
Think of my life-long sor-row ___ If you caught pneu-mo-nia and died ___

real - ly can't stay _____ Ah, but it's cold ___ out -
real - ly can't stay _____ Ah, but it's cold ___ out -

Oh, ba - by, don't hold ___ out, Ba - by, It's Cold ___ Out -
Get ov - er that old ___ doubt, Ba - by, It's Cold ___ Out -

1
side. ___

2.
I side. ___

side. ___ side. ___

pp

A Root'n Toot'n Santa Claus

Words & Music by Oakley Haldeman & Peter Tinturin

boys, _____ Git a long lit-tle rein deer Git a long: _____ Cov - er

all the range to night. _____ It's a long, long trail, An all night trail, But

you can bet your boots that San - ta won't fail: He's A ROO-T'N TOO-T'N

SAN - TA CLAUS. And he's on his mer - ry way, _____ He will round up all your

Christ-mas dreams, with a yip - py - yo ki - ya! _____ He's a _____

1.
B♭

2.
B♭

Happy Xmas (War Is Over)

Words & Music by John Lennon & Yoko Ono

young. _____

young. _____

A mer - ry, mer - ry

D   D(sus4)   D13

X - mas _____   And a hap - py New   year,   let's hope it's a

G   A   G   F#m

To Coda ⊕

good one _____   with - out an - y   fear.   And so this is

Em   G   D   E   E7

X - mas   for weak and for   strong   The rich and the

(War   is   o - ver   if   you   want   it

A   Amaj7   D6   A   Bm   Bm   Bm9   Bm
     (Ped E)   (7#)

Jingle Bells

Traditional

ride and sing a sleigh-ing song to - night. Oh,

Jin - gle bells, jin - gle bells, jin - gle all the

L.H.   L.H.

way, oh what fun it is to ride in a

one horse o - pen sleigh._____ one horse o - pen sleigh.

Mistletoe And Wine

Music by Keith Strachan
Words by Leslie Stewart & Jeremy Paul

passed, there's a new —— be - gin-ning. Dreams of San - ta,

dreams of snow, Fin - gers numb, fac - es a - glow. It's

Christ - mas time, mis-tle-toe and wine, Child - ren

sing - ing Chris - ti-an rhyme With logs on the fire —— and

gifts on the tree; A time to re - joice in the good that we

see. **2.** A time —— for liv - ing, a time for be - liev - ing, A

3.It's a time —— for giv - ing, a time for get - ting, A

time —— for trust-ing, not —— de - ceiv - ing.

time for —— for - giv-ing, and for —— for - get - ting.

Love and laugh - ter and joy ev - er af - ter;

Christ - mas is love, Christ - mas is peace; A

Ours for the tak-ing just fol-low —— the mas-ter. cease.
time for hat-ing and fight-ing to

Christ - mas time, mis-tle-toe and wine, child - ren sing - ing

Chris - ti - an rhyme With logs on the fire — and gifts on the

tree; A time to re - joice in the good that we see. see.

7/02 (44735)